Y0-BFK-200

Puppies for Sale: $25.00

To Rosie

Paws + Kisses

Rosalie Pope

Puppies for Sale: $25.00

A Collection of the Best Dog Stories Ever

Rosalie A. Pope

AuthorHouse™
1663 Liberty Drive
Bloomington, IN 47403
www.authorhouse.com
Phone: 1-800-839-8640

© 2011 by Rosalie A. Pope. All rights reserved.

No part of this book may be reproduced, stored in a retrieval system, or transmitted by any means without the written permission of the author.

First published by AuthorHouse   06/23/2011

ISBN: 978-1-4634-0932-6 (sc)
ISBN: 978-1-4634-0930-2 (ebk)

Library of Congress Control Number: 2011907942

Printed in the United States of America

Any people depicted in stock imagery provided by Thinkstock are models, and such images are being used for illustrative purposes only.

Certain stock imagery © Thinkstock.

This book is printed on acid-free paper.

Because of the dynamic nature of the Internet, any web addresses or links contained in this book may have changed since publication and may no longer be valid. The views expressed in this work are solely those of the author and do not necessarily reflect the views of the publisher, and the publisher hereby disclaims any responsibility for them.

Contents

For Xena, the best dog that ever lived.

Preface

There are a few people that come to mind as I write this book that must be thanked for the advice and guidance they gave me while I was making the decision to lay my Xena down. When I first got the news from the veterinarian that Xena had a tumor on her spleen, the first friend I called was Robin. We went to high school together, and she is still a sister to me. She recently had to put one of her six dogs down (yes, I said *six*), so I knew she would know how I felt at that very moment.

I called Robin almost every day, because I was very indecisive as to whether or not I should put Xena down yet. Xena was still having very good days and didn't seem to be in pain, but the fear was that the tumor would burst, and I wouldn't be home to help her. Each day, I called Robin crying to say, "Yes, I am going to do it," or "No, I'm not ready yet." This went on for almost two weeks. She made it clear to me that I had to do it for Xena, because I did not want her to go through pain. Thank you for being there for me and for understanding what I was going through. I love you.

Next is my friend Kellie, who not only hooked us up with our new dog Joe Joe, but gave me a phrase that I use over and over in this book and will continue to use for the rest of my life—and that is "we are Xena's people." Kellie works for the Nevada Humane Society in Reno. She is more sensitive to the needs of animals than she is to those of people. That is not a bad thing; she just happens to be a great pet lover and prefers pets over people. I had Kellie go over to my house to check on Xena. I had a big decision to make and wanted other opinions. She and our friend Nancy, a lover of all things pug, stayed with Xena for a little bit. While they were there, Xena began shaking as if she were really cold. She had done that earlier in the morning when my daughter Nikki was still home. I did not witness this. When I got home, Xena was her perfect normal self. We even took our walk together. There was no evidence of her being in pain. Crying, I called Kellie during our walk and said, "I just don't see what you are seeing."

She told me, "You won't see it, because you are her people." I immediately broke down. I had never heard pet ownership put in such a way. We were Xena's "people," and she would never show us how much in pain she really was. She was always happy to see us and be with us. That is why we didn't see it. At that moment, everything was clear. Thanks, Kellie, for sharing your tears and love for our beloved Xena. Thank you, Nancy, for calming Xena down when she was in need. You both are dear friends, and I will never forget what you did.

Griselda keeps me spiritually aware. We work together and share many experiences, both personally and professionally. Right after I got off the phone with Kellie, Griselda sent me a text that read, "You don't see what they see, because that's not how God wants you to remember her." Nothing more needed to be said.

My friend Bonnie, who has been our family friend for fifteen years, said, "Be strong for her. All she knows is happy. What a great life she's had." All of those messages received simultaneously and all of the prayers and wishes from friends all over gave me the strength to do right by my Xena. Thank you all, and if I haven't told you lately, I love you.

One very special person is Cathleen A. Green, DVM. She came to our home so that Xena could be in the place she loved the most when it was time to let her go. Thank you, Dr. Green, for doing what you do. They were very special moments for us, and being in our home with our precious girl for her final moments was absolutely priceless.

🐾x🐾

Last, but not least, to my husband, Bill, who often says no but always means yes. Thank you for never saying no and meaning it to any pet that has come into our home. You have the kindest heart, and I love you.

Introduction

I was recently told by a friend that our family has the best dog stories ever. I felt proud of that, but I soon wondered why everyone's stories aren't as great. Maybe they are. They just aren't as inclined to tell them as we are. We tell our dog stories to friends just as we tell our stories about our children. I started to think about all of the stories I had stored in my memory of the dogs we have owned. It brought such comfort to me at a time when I really needed to be lifted. I started writing this book one day after putting down the best dog that we have ever had. Xena Princess Warrior was just as her namesake implies. She had a mix of cocker spaniel, retriever, and maybe something else mixed in there. Those were the two obvious genetic traits you could see right away. After some research, my husband thinks that she may have been a field spaniel, although I think their ears are longer than what hers were.

Xena was tough, playful, exciting, adventurous, gentle, and beautiful. She was my shadow, my breath, and my heart, and when she died, I couldn't breathe. I lost a big part of me that warm, sunny day in January. I cried uncontrollably as if I had lost my best friend—and in fact, I did. I couldn't stop staring at the photos I had taken of Xena just the day before of our final walk together. One picture in particular struck me in such a way that I had to release my grief, and so I began writing about her. This is something I never felt the need to do before. The feeling to write about her was overpowering.

The picture was of Xena crossing our bridge that we have crossed hundreds of times together. She always walked a little bit ahead of me but always turned around to make sure that I was there. At that particular moment, she turned around, and I snapped the shot. What I got was a remarkable message from her from heaven. She was looking back at me with her tail straight up in the air, smiling as if she were still a puppy; the sun was shining on her, putting a brilliant glow around her furry frame. When I brought this up on my computer, I made it my background and stared at it for literally hours, sobbing. She was crossing the bridge, and this time, I would not be crossing with her, but the light behind her was letting me know that she is going to be okay. Her smile let me know she was going to be okay.

She was not just the Princess Warrior, she was our Xeenie Beans, Xeenie Weenie, Baby Girl, and My Little Fatness (my girl loved her snacks—and let's not forget the McDonald's french fries). These were names we also lovingly used to refer to her.

This book is to help me in my healing process and hopefully help others who grieve the loss of their pets just as deeply. It is heart-wrenching pain you feel when a pet is gone. Don't discount it just because they are animals. It is a true feeling that you are entitled to have. Take the time to mourn and heal. I felt silly at first leaving work early the next day, but every time someone came to me to try to console me, I just broke down in tears. It was crazy for me to think that I would be able to function at all so quickly. I gave into my own stubbornness, went home, and cried my heart out. Pets truly are gifts in our lives that should never be taken for granted. They are a part of our families and should always be treated with love and respect. I am writing this book, because I want everyone to know Xena; she is that worthy.

These stories about all of our dogs over the years are to provide comfort, laughter, sadness, joy, and a feeling of camaraderie to all of us who can relate in the trials and tribulations and most of all rewards of pet ownership. It is not always a bed of roses, just as it is not always a bed of roses to raise children. Really, there is no difference. We are responsible for their actions whether they are good or bad. We care for them when they are sick, discipline them when they are naughty, and love them regardless.

We are responsible for helping our pets hold on to their dignity even at the toughest time in their lives, which is their imminent death. This moment in time for a pet owner is by far the most difficult experience they will ever go through, but it can also be the most comforting to both the owner and the pet. Putting a dog down, when you do it in a way that is meaningful, will help in your healing process. For our family, it is very important that our pets are put down in their own home with everyone surrounding them who love them the most. Dr. Cathleen Greene, here in Reno, came to our home, and with compassion to the pet and to the owners, she helped with the process of putting our Xena down. I don't know how she can see the sadness every day, but she offers so much more than you would expect the experience to be.

Xena was put down in the middle of our living room floor on Wednesday, January 26, 2011, at 10:00 a.m. She was surrounded by her people that included Bill, her boy Adam, her girl Nikki, Adam's girlfriend Brenn, and me. We surrounded her with love, affection, and all of the treats she wanted to eat. We told her what a great dog she was and that we loved her most out of all of the others we have had. As we watched her slowly drift off to sleep, I lay on the floor cradling her body next to mine, her head resting on my arm, holding her tighter than I have ever held her before and crying with my head against her head into her shiny, reddish-brown fur. Everyone was a weeping mess, but Xena left this world to be in a better one and waits for our arrival so we may cross the Rainbow Bridge together.

I was fortunate to have time to spend with Xena in the morning before we put her down. We walked her favorite path and crossed her favorite bridge. She drank out of the freezing cold Truckee River and got her feet wet. She even tried finding animals under rocks. Her tail was held high, and she was on a hunt. Her smile was wide. She was a happy girl. That will always be how I remember her.\

"Rainbow Bridge"

There is a bridge connecting heaven and earth. It is called the Rainbow Bridge because of its many colors. Just this side of the Rainbow Bridge, there is a land of meadows, hills, and valleys with lush green grass.

When a beloved pet dies, the pet goes to this place. There is always food, water, and warm spring weather. The old and frail animals are young again. Those who are maimed are made whole again. They play all day with each other.

There is only one thing missing. They are not with their special person who loved them on earth. So, each day, they run and play until the day comes when one suddenly stops playing and looks up! The nose twitches! The ears are up! The eyes are staring, and this one suddenly runs from the group!

You have been seen, and when you and your special friend meet, you take him or her in your arms and embrace. Your face is kissed again and again, and you look once more into the eyes of your trusting pet.

Then you cross the Rainbow Bridge together, never again to be separated.

—Unknown author

1

Xena Princess Warrior

How Xena Found Her People

Xena came to us by pure luck. Bill and I went searching for a mate for our Akita, Sumo. (His story will follow.) Sumo was a big, beautiful, strong Akita. We never liked having just one dog in the house. We always felt that they needed companionship of their own kind when their person or people were not around. One Sunday, Bill, our son Adam, and I decided to go to the local pet store to see if they had any Akitas or if they knew any breeders. Sadly, the store was closed, and we drove away quite disappointed. Our hopes were to show up at the house and surprise Sumo with a new friend. Driving slowly out of the parking lot, we saw a woman who, with no exaggeration, looked like Cruella de Vil from the Disney movie *101 Dalmatians*. It was a cold March day. She had on a long, dark-colored fur coat that she was holding tightly closed to keep out the cold with one hand while smoking a cigarette with the other. She had the distinguishing white streak of long hair draped across her face and covering one eye and a large cardboard sign resting on a lawn chair sitting by her beat-up orange pickup truck that read, "Puppies for sale: $25.00."

My immediate reaction was to stop the car and make sure that they were not Dalmatians in the truck for fear that she would make a coat out of them if they were not purchased. Our hearts were truly set on getting a purebred Akita until we saw the many dogs in the bed of her pickup truck. It made me sad to see so many of them cold and crying. Some of them were playing with each other, and others were sitting alone, but I just recall thinking that there were so many of them that I wished I could take them all.

I asked the woman if it was okay if my son Adam—who was then seven years old—and I could get in the back of the truck to take a better look at the puppies. She agreed, and we both immediately jumped in the back. All of the dogs seemed to pounce on Adam with excitement. I wondered how we could ever choose which one to get. They were all so adorable and cuddly. I sat down on the tire wheel hump to watch him interacting with the dogs. He loved every lick and nip he was getting from each of the puppies. They swarmed him with their affection and playfulness. I enjoyed hearing his laughter. Within seconds of sitting down, one lonely dog walked away from the pack over to me, looked at me with her big, brown, beautiful eyes, and the rest is history. I remember that moment so vividly. I knew in an instant that this was my dog. Xena found me that day and changed our lives forever. I took one look at her beautiful little face and immediately told my husband, "I don't want to look any further. This is our new dog." She found her own people. We elatedly drove home with her licking our faces every bit of the way, and her tail never stopped wagging.

Sumo and Xena Meet

Sumo excitedly greeted us at the door as he usually did. This time, there was something different. There was something in my arms that piqued his interest. I held Xena tightly at first and let Sumo settle his curiosity by allowing him to come to me and sniff her while she was in my arms. I wasn't sure how he would react to a new puppy and wanted to be sure that she was safe. When we all felt comfortable that Sumo would behave, I put Xena down on the floor. After they did the customary sniff and greet that only dogs know how to do, it was obvious that they took an instant liking to each other. Sumo instantaneously towered over her, put his entire mouth over her little head, and began drooling all over her, gently chewing on her as if she were a new chew toy. Rather than being fearful of this big, bad Akita, she broke away, charged him, and started chewing on his ear while jumping all over him, hence the name Xena Princess Warrior. It took no time at all for us to realize who she needed to be named after. She had no fear, and since we were big fans of the TV character, naming her was a no-brainer. She lived up to that name every day of her life.

And Then There Were Four

Advancing time a year, we had not gotten Xena fixed yet, and Sumo wanted to try to make babies with her. He was not fixed, either, because we always wanted to breed him. We still had the hopes of having another Akita in our home. Well, things change, and we decided to get him fixed, because we did not want puppies, and he was determined to try *all the time!* We made the appointment with the vet, got Sumo fixed, and we thought that was that—no more worries. We saw him trying to do the humpty hump with her just one day after his surgery. We were a bit shocked at his actions, but we were not worried. He was fixed, and again, that was the end of that.

A few months went by. I was home alone with my son, who was having a sleepover with four other boys who were all about nine years old at this time. I was pregnant with my daughter Nikki, and my husband was working the swing shift at the hotel. Xena began following me more closely than she normally did. I noticed her panting extremely heavily and just clinging to me wherever I went. She was literally following me around like she was a lost puppy dog. I told Adam, "I hope nothing is wrong with her," and we started petting her while keeping a close eye. Her panting reminded me of birth, since I had been through that process once myself and was getting ready to do it again. It seemed familiar, but there was no way she was pregnant, because Sumo was fixed.

All of a sudden, in the dining room of our house, Xena plopped out this big blob of goo, and all of the boys started screaming when they saw her starting to lick and eat the goo off the ball-like blob that was now lying on the floor.

"*Eww!* Eww! That's gross! What is that?" they all screamed. "Why is she eating it?" Imagine my dilemma. Now, not only was my dog having puppies while my son had four boys over, I had to help keep her calm, the boys calm, deliver puppies, and explain what just happened to a bunch of nine-year-old boys—and let's not forget that I would have to tell my husband that he was a grandfather.

As I picked up my jaw from the floor, I tried to immediately calm the boys down so they wouldn't scare Xena. I quickly ran to get towels and blankets to set up an emergency delivery room in the bathroom. I gently picked up the puppy from the floor with one of the towels. With Xena keeping a very close, watchful eye on me holding her new baby, I guided Xena to what would become her new birthing place. I had already called my husband to not only wish him a happy birthday (yes, it was his birthday), but to congratulate him on becoming a grandfather. After explaining to Bill about the night's exciting events, he was in disbelief. However, his disbelief was not my concern at that particular point. I told him that I would call later, because I had puppies to deliver.

So, picture this—four boys in a small bathroom, one pregnant mother-to-be, and one dog we didn't even know was pregnant delivering puppies sitting on the bathroom floor patiently waiting for the next delivery. We surrounded Xena, comforting her, petting her, and letting her do her thing. The boys were still thinking and deeply discussing viewing the blob that came out of her in the dining room. Boys can be very descriptive during times like these, and I dare say they lack sensitivity. They did not actually see it come out, so imagine their surprise when puppy number two came out. The realization of seeing where it actually came out hit them—or I should say where they *perceived* it to come from. Again, they began with the "Ewws" and "Oh, that's gross" comments.

While I was trying to keep them calm so Xena would stay calm—and mind you, I was pretty far along in my pregnancy—my son blurts out, "Gross, Mom, are you going to poop out the baby from your butt hole when she comes out?" I wish I could make that statement a bit less graphic for this book, but that is what he blurted out. A bit embarrassed, but hysterically laughing, I again picked up my jaw from the floor and explained that it is not where the baby comes out. I didn't want to go into detail at that point, and I told the boys to ask their parents about it. I didn't feel I should take that privileged experience of explaining the facts of life away from their own parents, although the boys did sort of get a crash course that night.

The second puppy came out, and thankfully, that was all Xena had. They were huge, and I couldn't believe my baby, who was still a puppy herself, had just pushed them out. I had a real "I am woman, hear me roar" moment. If Xena could do that twice, then I could do that once. That's my Warrior.

The lesson to be learned here is that even though you get your dog fixed so they can't make babies, keep them apart for a day or two to make sure that all of the baby juice is out of their systems. The last bit of baby juice left in Sumo created the cutest puppies. One of the puppies looked exactly like Sumo—fat and furry with a big head but with Xena's straight tail—and the other looked just like Xena with reddish-brown hair but with Sumo's curly tail. It couldn't have been cuter or sweeter than that. I called Billy to give him an update. When he came home, we were all still awake and watching Xena becoming the best mommy to her pups. We named the pups Hampshire (because he was as big as a baby pig) and Spaz because she was just a bit crazy.

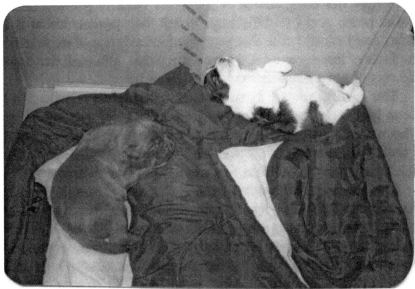

Like a Little Puppy Dog

As Xena was getting used to her new home and her new family, she grew very close to me. I am not saying that she did not love everyone else—because she did, very much—but she began following me all over the house. She slept on top of my pillow, just barely touching my head. She would alternate between Bill and me, but she always had to be near. As she grew older, our bond just kept getting closer and closer. It grew more after Sumo was gone. I always felt guilty if we took one dog someplace and not the other, so we usually did not do much with them outside of the house. Since they had an acre of land to play around in, we were not too worried. When Sumo had passed, my relationship with Xena changed forever. It was when she truly became more than my pet. She became my best friend.

When I got home from work each night, I came home to loud, ear-piercing barking and excited whining (I like to say that she was singing with happiness). She would not calm down until I put down my bags and purse and petted her until she was satisfied; this routine sometimes lasting several minutes. It was like she was giving me grief for not being home with her all day. Conversations with me could not be had until Princess was at peace. Her excitement when I got home was so loud that you couldn't hear what anyone was trying to say to you. Although she did act excited when everyone else came home, it was more to the extreme when I walked through the door. From the moment I came home to the moment I went to bed, Xena was by my side always. This became our routine for the rest of her life.

I began taking her everywhere with me. She was my running buddy, my movie-watching, popcorn-eating buddy, Frisbee golf buddy, cooking buddy (actually, food-sampling buddy), mountain-climbing buddy . . . wherever I went, she went. I would have it no other way.

There was such a bond that I had never had with any other dog in my entire life. They were all loved and special to me, but none can compare to my Xena. I was never lonely when she was by my side. I can explain it no other way but to say it again that she was my shadow and my breath. When she passed, I felt that I could no longer breathe. A couple of weeks have passed now since Xena left this earth, and I still find myself getting teary eyed at any moment. Usually on the ride home from work, I think about going for a run before making dinner and taking her with me. Now, I go alone or just don't go at all, and it makes me sad. I keep telling myself that it is okay to grieve. Writing and remembering the stories we created together is giving me comfort that I cannot find anywhere else.

Bird, Bird, Bird

One of Xena's favorite pastimes for sure was her love of catching a bird midair. She could chase birds all day long, and when she got one, she was always very proud of her catch. She eagerly brought them into the house, dropping them at our feet—usually while we were in the kitchen making dinner. When she was in that mode, you could just hear her obsessive thoughts, which was only one word: *bird, bird, bird*. You could almost hear her think it.

One day, Adam came home from school with some of his buddies. We had a large, three-piece sectional couch with two reclining chairs that they all could fit on. They were comfortably playing video games as they did quite often. Bill and I were at work. Xena came into the house with a bird and proudly laid it by Adam's feet. The boys were a bit grossed out. They created a frenzy by screaming, and the bird got away. Nobody saw where the bird went, and the boys followed Xena and ran outside. When the boys went outside, they left the reclining chairs open.

Xena, by this time, was going wild and was back in the house looking by the couch where the bird was last seen. She ran around the couch in a frenzied sort of way, panting and going back and forth. Adam called me at work sounding panicked. He told me about the bird. He said they couldn't find it, but Xena was going nuts, and he didn't know what to do. I worked right down the street and immediately rushed home. Just as Adam described, Xena was very energized and was in hunting form. Her pointed nose was stuck on the couch; her stance was that of a dog that was ready for the kill. Her tail stood straight on end with every bit of her long fur feathered out from the rise. We could not figure out what she was looking for, and as far as the boys knew, the bird went out the door. I searched and searched the couch and found nothing and heard nothing. I had to go back to work, and the boys were also leaving to play outside. I phoned Bill and told him what was going on. He said he would look when he got home.

A couple of hours passed. I entered our home, and when I came out of my kitchen and saw the incredible destruction of my once beautiful blue couch, I stood there in disbelief. Xena had chewed every part of the reclining part of the chair as well as the whole back of the couch. Foam and fabric were strewn all over the living room. I did not call Bill. I figured I would let him experience the surprise, too. Xena was still steadfast in her attempt to find whatever she was looking for. It appeared she was unsuccessful at this point in retrieving her hunt. She spotted me staring at her and quickly came over for a brief hello. She then swiftly went back to her post and continued the frantic behavior, looking at me as if she wanted me to see something in the couch.

Adam came home with the other boys, and in unison, they gasped, their voices raised in utter shock. We all gathered around the destruction, and for a quick second, I heard something. I shushed the boys, waiving my hand in an effort to get them to be silent. We waited. There it was again—a fluttering sound coming from the couch. Xena began singing her high-pitched song of excitement, and she had an "I told you so" quality about it this time.

I began looking for the bird, and at that time, Bill walked in, and all you heard was a loud, deep voice yell, "Oh, my God!"

I told him we had just heard the bird. Xena was going crazy. We heard it again, and Bill said, "It is inside the couch." The boys left the recliners up, and the bird ran in the opening and played dead for hours until we heard the flutter. Bill flipped what was left of the couch over and began cutting into it. At this point, it didn't really matter; the couch was history. He saw the bird, and it was still. He thought it was dying. Little did we know that the bird was playing dead for real. He was able to grab it, and he brought it out wrapped in a towel. Xena was salivating at this point. Her hopes were that we were going to hand the prize over to her. She was doing her happy dance, stepping back and forth on each paw over and over, licking her lips, smiling her big smile and panting heavily. She was soon disappointed. Bill took the bird outside and let it go. Fortunately and unbelievably, the bird was not hurt. It was more scared than anything.

As we stood there surrounding the remnants of our couch, all I kept saying was, "Xena, Xena, Xena." It finally clicked in for her that what she did was not a good thing. Mom and Dad were not happy campers right then. She looked at me with her head down now, looking up at me with her sad puppy eyes that were rolled to the top of her forehead. There was a slight smile on her face, and she was still panting as she recovered from the excitement. I took one look at her, shook my head, got on the floor, and gave her the biggest hug and kiss while telling her that I loved her and that it was okay. "It's okay, Baby Girl. It's okay."

Swim, Xena, Swim

I never knew Xena liked the water until we moved. There is a marina across the street that has a dog park and a walking path that goes all the way around it. It is a two-mile walk, so it was great exercise for both of us. We looked forward to our walk together every day. She excitedly began her barking when I got home, because she knew we walked before anything else was done. We always stopped to let her off the leash and run in the dog park. There were always ducks in the water swimming and taunting her. Xena chased the ducks and sometimes would swim to try to catch one. Thankfully, she never did catch one, although she did come close several times.

One particular visit to the park brings back fond memories. She must have been feeling a bit feisty on that day, because she seemed to have a lot of energy. Kellie and I sat on the bench that I always sat on and began watching her be a dog. She ran up and down the beach area, smelled her fair share of the grassy areas, and pretty much ignored all of the other dogs just as she always had. She was always somewhat of a loner in that sense. The other dogs would immediately spot her as we walked into the park, and they would run up to her and begin their greeting rituals. She just ignored them as she did the day we met her when she walked away from the pack; she never really played with other dogs, and they would run off and play elsewhere.

Suddenly, she took the warrior stance of attack. I followed my eyes along her line of sight to see what she was looking at so intently. Waiting in the water not far away was a flock of ducks just sitting in the water, bating her. Come and get us! Come and get us! Kellie noticed this too, and said, "Xena, go get the ducks." I quickly yelled at Kellie, "Don't tell her that!." I knew what was about to happen. All of a sudden, Xena's thoughts became *duck, duck, duck*. Seem familiar? She tore after those ducks like a bolt of lightning and swam her little heart out.

The ducks swam fast to get away, but they kept a teasing pace just out of her reach. Usually, she would swim a little way out, give up, and then turn around. This particular swim was never ending. She was so fixated on the ducks that she did not hear me screaming for her to come back. She was almost to the middle of the marina, which was quite a ways away. I started panicking, calling her frantically. She was so far out and still had to swim back. I was afraid that she would be too tired to finish. Other people came over and watched with Kellie and me, and they, too, started calling her. They couldn't believe that she was still going. She was so fixated on the ducks that she was not aware of anything else around her.

Finally, I called her, and she looked back. She then did a double take as if to say, "Holy crap, Batman, I am really far away. I'd better get back." Her double take was priceless, and the poor thing swam her little heart out. It was really windy that day. The wind made currents in the water and kept pushing

Xena further to the side. The strength of the currents was making it really hard for her to swim back. She was exhausted when she finally got to shore. All of the onlookers cheered her on, saying, "Come on, Xena!" When she did finally reach shore, they cheered and clapped for her. Needless to say, we went straight home and did not finish our walk that day. She plopped right on the floor and was out like a light; that is, after she made sure she got her treat, of course. My little athlete was pooped out.

2

Sumosan

Our big, beautiful Akita was Sumo. Sumosan was his given name, because when he was a puppy, he was the fattest of the litter. His chest was broad, and his paws were pigeon-toed. He looked like a sumo wrestler when he stood still. Bill and I instantly fell in love with him. He became a great protector of our family and was just a big gentle giant of a dog. To those who knew him, he wouldn't hurt anyone—that is, as long as they were human. Other animals outside the home were totally a different story.

Spaghetti and Skunk Sauce

We used to live out of the city limits, and the neighborhood was separated by one—to two-acre parcels. Most of the people on our block had one acre, and some had horses, goats, sheep, rams, and even llamas. There were always bunnies around the front yard, and at night, you would smell skunks or see raccoons running around looking for food. We always hated the skunks, because no matter what we tried to do to prevent them from coming in our yard, they always managed to get in—and every year, Sumo would always be the one to get skunked.

More often than not, the skunking occurred at night. We would have to lock him out of the house, and Bill would have to give Sumo his skunk removal bath with his recipe of Murphy's Oil Soap, Tegrin Medicated Shampoo, lemon juice, and Arm & Hammer baking soda. (It works like a charm; he swears by it.)

Winter skunkings were the worst, because it was so cold, and the water from the outside hose was freezing. Bill was a trooper and took care of Sumo right away. He never made him stay outside or wait until the morning.

One particular evening brings back hysterically funny memories. Not that the skunkings were ever funny, but we take exception to this story. I was working late one evening. I arrived home around 6:30 or 7:00 p.m. Our very dear family friend Bonnie came over and was going to have dinner with us. We were going to attend the balloon races the following morning at 5:30 a.m., so Bonnie was going to sleep on the couch in our living room.

I was on my homemade spaghetti kick and began making it with my machine. We were all relaxing and having some wine and talking in the kitchen while Bill was watching TV. We had a great room, and the kitchen was opened up to look right in it. Bonnie and I were absolutely starving. It was later than we usually ate, so our hunger pangs were growing and getting loud.

As we were relaxing and enjoying our conversation and wine, I began stirring the sauce, and that's when chaos ensued. Sumo came charging through the doggie door coughing, hacking, and sneezing like I have never seen before. He was almost blindly looking for some relief as he entered the kitchen, violently sneezing and spewing snot and red stuff everywhere. Bonnie, having had one too many glasses of wine, wondered how Sumo had gotten sauce when I was just stirring it. We didn't realize at the time that it was skunk blood. I panicked and tried to grab him. As I got closer and almost at the same time, Bonnie and I simultaneously got a whiff of the strongest skunk odor we have ever smelled. Sumo had gotten sprayed! He was sneezing in the kitchen next to my beautiful homemade pasta. He shook his large furry head from left to right over and over, attempting to get the smell out of his own breath, and wetness flew out from his nose and mouth. The stench was suffocating.

We all grabbed our faces with the hope of masking some of the odor, but our attempts were futile. The stench was already in our mouths and in our noses. There was no escaping the horrific odor. Our eyes burned; we choked from the smell and had to go outside for fresh air. All of a sudden, Bill grabbed Sumo and locked him outside, blocking the doggie door so that he couldn't get back in. It didn't matter, because the damage was already done. The house, our clothes, our shoes, our hair—everything was "skunkified."

These events happened so fast. As the excitement began to settle and poor Bill bathed Sumo in the cold fall air, Bonnie and I remembered that we were still starving. By this time, it was around 9:00 p.m. I put on the spaghetti. When Bill came in and saw us eating in the stinky kitchen, he couldn't believe that we could still eat with the skunk taste in our mouths and in our noses. I did clean the kitchen before we made the spaghetti, but the odor was still lingering all over the house. We were hungry. What can I say?

The house reeked so badly that Bill could not stay in the living room, let alone eat my delicious spaghetti. His stomach was not as tough as ours—or maybe he'd just lost his appetite. He retreated to the bedroom where the odor was absent, and Bonnie and I continued to dine on spaghetti and skunk sauce.

The kicker of this story is that the odor lingered in the house for two weeks. There was no relief. I went to work, and wherever I went, the odor went. I later realized that it was on my shoes from walking on my carpet. I could smell it in my car, under my desk, just everywhere.

Bonnie went home that night, because the odor was just overpowering. She tried to quietly climb into bed and not wake her sleeping husband, but he suddenly woke up and asked her what kind of perfume she was wearing, because it smelled like skunk. She told him the story, and for the next two weeks, her house smelled like skunk, too, and everywhere she went, the smell followed her, too. I believe she even slept on the couch that night at her own house.

A Little Bit of Mutton Never Hurt Anyone

Now, not all of our stories are funny—at least, not while they were happening. Some were pretty darn stressful. We even thought about giving Sumo away a time or two. We just could never do it, and fortunately, our neighbors never made us.

Our yard was large, and we had a six-foot fence around the perimeter. There was no way Sumo or any other dog we had could get out—or so we thought. One day, one of our neighbors came to our door and said that he had seen Sumo at the house located down the street with the llamas and sheep. Sumo had gotten out and decided to visit them. He killed the sheep and hurt the ram so badly that they had to put the ram down. We were horrified. How can this gentle giant become so vicious?

The next day, I went to the neighbors' house to apologize, and I offered to pay for any vet bills or damages. They were so incredibly nice even though they were grieving. They had to put down the ram, and to comfort me, they said that Sumo was just doing what dogs do. I had visions in my head of Sumo having to be put down, too. I cried with them. The ram cost us $500, and they agreed to let us make payments.

Sumo also hurt a Rottweiler that lived somewhere in the neighborhood. To this day, I am not sure whose dog that was. Although these events were terrible, as we look back at them and recount the events through our storytelling, Sumo comes out looking like such a bad-ass dog. Those were not proud moments, but the time the police came knocking on my door because my son decided to graffiti someone's yard wasn't, either. The things we put up with from our kids. I didn't put him down. They do make for great storytelling later, though.

Tag Teaming

So, I guess you are wondering just how Sumo got out of the fence. It turns out that he had an accomplice, and it was none other than the Princess Warrior herself. Xena loved to dig holes. We used to find them all over the yard. She was usually chasing the voles, squirrels, or something. We found them usually by falling into them. Little did we know that she was digging holes at the base of the fence. We caught her digging one day with Sumo supervising over her shoulder.

We stood back to see what he would do, and don't you know he tried to push through the fence where she was digging. She would dig, stop, and then step back as if she were taking a look at her handiwork just as a painter would to view his painting. Sumo stepped in and pushed the fence first with his nose and then with his large paw. He realized that it was a no-go. You could just see his little brain working. He couldn't get out that way, so he'd have to find another way out.

He looked toward the sky as if he were getting a message from God. The message was to climb the fence, and so that is what Sumo did. This large, one-hundred-pound dog climbed as if he were about one day old and was just learning how to use his legs. Each step was slowly and methodically placed so that no errors would be made. One leg would shake as he moved the other leg up a rung. He looked so awkward. Bill and I stood back and watched the show. It was quite funny. Sumo made it to the top just in time to feel the defeat. Bill caught him just as he reached the top and pulled him back down. Sumo knew that he was caught in the act. He instantly hung his head low as if to say, "Darn, I got caught again." He was so close to success, yet so far away. We had to start tethering him until we fixed the fence so that he couldn't leave the yard. Xena, for the record, never tried to leave. She just loved digging the holes.

Take Me to the Treats

A.K.A. Wally Wally Bing Bangs

One of the cutest things Sumo used to do was to take us to his treats. As soon as we walked in the door from work and gave him his first pets for the evening, he would gently grab our hands with his mouth and pull us to his treat jar. We never taught him how to do this. Just one day, he started to do it on his own. Our dear friend Janet was a sucker for Sumo, and when she came in, she automatically went to the treat jar and gave him some.

One day, she came over and forgot to give him a treat. Sumo was going to nip that behavior right in the bud. He grabbed her hand gently with his wet, drooling mouth and guided her in front of the cookie-filled jar. She asked him, "What do you want from me?" This was new to her, too. Akitas are not barkers by nature, and he gave her one deep woof in response to her question and looked at the treat jar. She could not believe it. He didn't do that for any other friends but Janet. She had him so spoiled.

From that day on, Janet never just walked in and gave him his treat. He now had to work for it and lead her. It's funny, because none of us ever minded getting our hands slobbered on by Sumo. We looked forward to that.

I don't know why, but we started to call his treats "wallies." Wallies later became "wally wally bing bangs." Every time we wanted to get his attention, we always said, "Wally wally bing bang," and he would cock his head to the side and perk up his ears. His eyes would go wide, and he would go straight to the kitchen for a treat. To this day, we still call dog treats "wallies." It is funny how some things just stick like that. All of the dogs after Sumo get just as excited when they hear the word "wally."

Time to Rest Our Gentle Giant

We had our beloved Sumo for twelve great years. People tell us that it is a pretty long life for an Akita, so we feel blessed that he wanted to be with us for so long. We knew it was time to put Sumo down when his suffering was obvious. He began losing his bowels in the house, which he never did before. You could see his shame when this occurred, because his head was down, and he came to us for reassurance. We would guide him outside and of course give him any comfort he needed. He also had hip dysplasia, which is very common in large dogs. It was easy to know when to put Sumo down, because the signs were obvious. We wanted him to keep his dignity and knew what we had to do.

Driving to the vet to put him down was a very sad experience. We left Adam home, because he would not be able to handle seeing his dog like that. He is my sensitive boy, and I didn't want to see him hurt that way.

Sumo's final car ride brought back some life even if it was for only the three miles it took to get there. Sumo loved the car. When we first bought him, he could not jump in by himself. We always had to lift him up until he got used to it. This time, we had to lift him up, not because he didn't know how, but because he lacked the strength to do it himself.

When the time came, the doctor gave Sumo his sleeping shot, and we continued to feed him all of the treats he could eat. The shot began working. Slowly, he fumbled with the treats as he began to lie down; he could no longer stand due to the drowsy feeling that was overcoming him. He had the biggest furriest head that you just could not help grabbing and loving. It overflowed in your hands. Bill and I took our turns loving that big fur ball and holding him tightly until he slipped away into a permanent slumber. Sumo was a good dog to the very end.

3

Nana

Talk about a beautiful dog and Nana comes to our minds. After we put down the gentle giant, another gentle giant entered our lives. We knew we wanted to have a companion for Xena. We didn't want her to be alone. Again, our thoughts were to find another Akita. This was just not meant to be. A friend of mine turned me on to a rescue center in California not too far from our home called High Sierra Animal Rescue. I got on their website and found the prettiest St. Bernard. I went home that night and told Bill that I'd found our new dog. He asked if it was an Akita, and I said no, but it was the prettiest St. Bernard. I immediately got on the Internet to show him, but not before he rolled his eyes, as usual. *Here we go again, bringing yet another dog into our lives.*

That weekend, we drove to Portola, California, to the rescue center. It was love at first sight. When the handler brought her out, we all fell in love and wanted her instantly. She was a huge, golden-brown St. Bernard. She truly looked like the Nana dog in the cartoon *Peter Pan*. There was just no question that she was to go home with us that day.

Put Your Head on My Table

Nana fit in right away. When we were sitting at the table during dinnertime, it was not unusual for the dogs to be sitting on the floor next to us, hoping for a small morsel. I know some people don't like that, but our dogs are our family, too, and dining together means just that. Nana was so big that her head was higher than our dinner table. She would stand next to Bill and put her head on the corner of the table and look at him with her droopy, expecting eyes. Let's not forget—she was a St. Bernard, and with those types of dogs, you get lots of drool. Dinnertime always produced the two-sided mouth drool. Long, gooey drool strands hung from either side of her mouth. It was gross, but it cracked us all up each time. We always had extra napkins at the dinner table for her.

Nana proved herself useful right away to Xena. There was a benefit to having such a large dog in the home, and Xena loved Nana for a couple of reasons. If we left any kind of food on the counter, Xena was always the first to know exactly where it was. I think she would tell Nana to grab it. With Xena standing next to her, Nana would sneak over and slyly reach up and grab whatever she could. Many times, it would drop to the floor. Of course, Xena was there to take her share. She never missed her opportunity to snag food. They were partners in crime. I never saw Nana physically jump up on the counter to get the food. I did witness her putting her head on the counter and turning it in such a way that it would give her neck an extension long enough to reach whatever there was to grab. We quickly learned to put the food away as soon as we were done.

Snowplow

One winter, we had a snowfall that was as high as my hips. Xena was not a tall dog, so it towered over her. Nana was so big that she plowed through the snow, making clear pathways for Xena. When they explored the yard after the heavy snow, Xena followed Nana in her path wherever she decided to go, making Nana do all of the hard work. It was a really cute sight to see. They both enjoyed the snow very much. It's always more fun when you have a friend to share it with.

The more I think about these stories that involve Xena, the more I realize how my girl was the brains behind all that was. Digging holes for Sumo, telling Nana where the food was, making Nana plow through the snow first so that she would walk behind her with little effort . . . hmmm, I see her a bit differently in retrospect, and it makes me love her more and more.

Not Enough Time

Nana was only five years old when we adopted her. We only had the pleasure of having her in our home for about a year and a half. She ended up getting cancer in her shoulder. It seemed to come on suddenly, and within a few weeks, she couldn't even walk. One day, I saw her using the wall to walk down our hallway. When I saw that, I knew it was her time. They suffer in silence and so bravely. Unfortunately, you don't know when it is time until it is physically evident. This was the first time we knew about Dr. Green's services, and we asked her to come to our home to put our pet down.

It was a warm April Saturday. Nana loved the yard, and so that is where we wanted her to be. It was a bit of a slow struggle getting her to go outside, but we knew it would be worth the effort for her once she got there. A big blanket was put on the grass. Bill, Nikki, and I were there. Adam was not ready to see it. He came by to give her kisses and hugs. With tears in his eyes, he then walked away. Nikki was very young and didn't really know what was going on. She was comforting in a sense, because while we were with Nana, Nikki roamed around us in her little Tinker Bell costume that she wore all the time, waving her Tinker Bell wand in hand, singing songs, and marching around us. It was quite cute and just what we needed. To her, Nana was just going to sleep.

We petted Nana, loved her, and treated her just as we did with Sumo and Xena. As she went to sleep, we could see the incredible pain of the cancer that she had been suffering from just disappear. Although it was yet another heartbreaking few moments to endure, her relief provided us comfort. We knew it was the right thing to do and felt at peace.

4

Marley

Marley, Marley, Marley . . . where do I even begin with this one? Of all of the dogs we have ever had, Marley (named after Bob Marley) is by far the most athletic. Marley is a strong, healthy, blue pit bull my son adopted as his first pet. Adam was living in his first apartment and wanted a dog of his own to keep him company. When he told me that he wanted a pit bull, I highly fought against it, not because of the breed but because he lived in an apartment, and most in this area would not allow them on the property. We owned pits ourselves. They are loving and friendly pets who truly have a bad reputation. Their bad reputations stem from having horrid owners who abuse them and train them to be violent.

Adam worked in an apartment community. It was the only one that allowed this breed. I told him that if he had a change in his job or if something happened that he couldn't control, he would have to get rid of the dog, so why even go there? It was heartbreak ready to happen. After all, what do I know—I am just his mother, right? There was no stopping him; he wanted this dog.

He found someone on Craigslist who was selling pit bull puppies. I went with him to make sure that he wasn't going to get a sick dog. We went to a small apartment located in a not-so-good neighborhood. Entering the apartment, I instantly smelled the urine. It was dirty. The man took Adam to see the puppies. Marley locked eyes with Adam, and Adam melted like butter. He said, "Mom, this is my dog." I have never seen him as excited as he was that moment. This dog was to be his companion hopefully for a long time. I told the man that I wanted to take the dog to the vet that was literally right around the corner to make sure that it was healthy. He agreed, and we all drove there. Marley was in good health, and the deal was done. Marley had found a new home with lots of love.

When It Rains, It Pours

The first couple of weeks that Marley lived with Adam were definitely the time the two would get to know each other. I advised Adam to get a crate to put Marley in while he was not at home. Training would take time, and we didn't want him to do any damage. Adam said that he didn't need it. "Marley is a good dog, Mom," he said. "He hasn't had any accidents or chewed anything." (Again, what do I know?) A couple of days into their relationship, Adam came knocking on our door at eleven o'clock at night. We only lived a few minutes away. We had just gone to bed and heard the frantic knocking.

Adam said that he'd gone to a party, and when he came home, his entire apartment was flooded. He had locked Marley in the bathroom, because he did not get a crate for him, and Marley had chewed the toilet line and flooded everything. In his frantic state of mind, Adam did not think of turning off the water to the toilet before coming to our house, so it was still flowing when we got there.

When we opened the door, all I saw was an ocean of water floating above my ankles, and all Adam's belongings were just soaked. Marley was really freaked out, and his tail was tightly tucked between his legs. The water was literally flowing off the third-floor balcony. We rushed to turn off the water to the toilet. We called our other maintenance guy, and he kindly came over to help. It was already after midnight at this point, and we were not making any progress getting the water out. It would have to wait until the morning.

The following morning, our carpet guy came over and took care of Adam's carpet by extracting the water. Adam had to pay for the cleaning of the carpet and the damaged waterline. He learned a very valuable lesson, and the next day, Marley was in a crate.

Catch Me If You Can

I don't want to say "I told him so," but Adam's job was changing, which meant that he had to move to another apartment. Of course, pit bulls were not allowed there. He sat across from me at my desk in the office with his big brown eyes and said, "Mom, would you be willing to keep Marley for me?" Of course, I can't bear breaking his heart, and after a deep sigh, I said that I would. After all, Marley was our first grandchild, and we grew to love him. Bill was not too happy about it. What was I going to do? Certainly not get rid of him. That was not an option.

It definitely took some getting used to Marley's ways. His high energy was a challenge to say the least. Xena was older and mellower, and now we had this tornado running through our home all the time.

We could see right off the bat that he was going to be a troublemaker. For the first few months, he did okay. Xena played well with him, and she certainly put him in his place when he bugged her as only Xena could. They played in the yard, and he loved to run back and forth along the fence as people walked by with their dogs. This did drive us crazy a bit, because he would bark at them like crazy, but it was not really a major deal.

One day, I got a call at work from my friend who lived three houses down. Apparently, Marley was out all afternoon terrorizing the neighborhood. As she continued to describe his activities, she pointed out that Marley was a "freakin' athlete." He jumped over the back part of our fence that leads to the driveway, and then he continued to cross the street to our neighbors' house. He jumped their six-foot fence and then jumped over their next-door neighbors' fence and walked through their front yard. But wait, there's more. Keep in mind that the surrounding neighbors are older. He walked in the house of our neighbor who happened to have her door opened. Sitting on her couch was her ninety-year-old mother. Imagine their surprise when a big pit bull ran through their house. Obviously, animal control was called. Luckily, our neighbor with the ninety-year-old mother didn't know that he was our dog, and we were only given a warning notice.

Marley jumped the fence a few more times and went into our neighbors' yard directly next door to us. They keep their dogs locked up in the garage, and he hears them barking all day. We have had to drag him out on more occasions than we would like to remember. One time, Bill forgot that he had Marley out there. Marley didn't come when called, so Bill followed the tether only to find Marley hanging by his harness on the other side of the fence. Thank goodness Marley was not wearing the neck collar. Marley now has to be tethered to a tree whenever he is in the yard with his harness on. Until we can come up with another solution, it is the way it will have to be.

On January 1, 2011, Bill and I were enjoying a cup of coffee and playing a game on the Internet as we usually do each day.

It was about 6:30 a.m., and all was quiet in the house. That is, until we heard barking. Bill forgot to close the doggie door when he let Xena out. All of a sudden, we heard barking under our window. It was Xena and Marley. This was not good, since the tethered dog should have been on the other side of the house. We would not normally hear him so close. Bill jumped up, remembering that the door was open. Sure enough, Marley jumped the fence, because a man was walking his dog right by our yard. He got him back quickly, thank goodness, and no harm was done—or so we thought.

Around three o'clock that afternoon, we put the dogs out. This time, Marley was tethered with the collar around his neck. Normally, he is in a harness, but it seemed to be giving him a rash, so we gave him a break and took it off for a while. Both Bill and I just happened to walk out of our garage—which was open—and to our surprise, what do we see? It was none other than the all-too-familiar animal control vehicle pulling into our driveway. Forgetting what happened at six thirty that morning, I was upset that they were there. Marley was innocent this time—plus he was now tethered in the yard. She could see for herself. He hasn't done anything! I was already claiming his innocence, and I had no idea why they were there.

I ran in the house for a minute to check that he was indeed still tethered. The animal control officer got out of the truck, and Bill began speaking with her. She explained that the gentleman walking his dog that morning had called about Marley jumping the fence. I was in the yard when they were talking, and as they approached the back of the fence, Marley spotted a man walking two dogs by our yard without leashes. He bolted with such force to the other end of the yard that he broke his collar off and flew right over the fence. To the man's surprise, all he could say was "Whoa!" The leap stopped him in his tracks. Marley was so fast and light that if you blinked you would miss the jump.

I screamed, "Oh, crap! Bill, he broke off the leash and jumped the fence!" Right in front of the animal control lady! Of all times for that to happen, seriously, what are the chances? I ran so fast out the gate and frantically tried to catch Marley.

He was running away from me as if he were running from the law—which he was, when you think about it. All he wanted to do was play with the dogs. He was so fast. I couldn't catch him, and he wouldn't sit still. The guy walking his dogs kept walking, and Marley was going with them. I asked the guy to please stand still so that I could grab Marley. He had no leash on. The only thing I could do was to pick up this eighty-pound dog by myself. Bill was not there yet, and I had no choice. I grabbed him under his front chest, and with half of his body dangling between my legs, I scampered to put him back in the yard. I apologized to the guy, and he was nice about it, but he did comment on how Marley came out of nowhere and literally flew over the fence. I know that would scare the heck out of me if that happened.

So now that it was over, we had to face the animal control lady. How the heck could we get out of that one? I played it well, though. I came out acting so angry that people walk by our yard day in and day out with their dogs off their leashes. I explained how that drives all of the dogs along this path crazy. Bill played it cool and tried to keep me calmed down.

The animal control officer said that she did see the guy that walked by and also saw that Marley was tethered. We explained about the harness, and she said to make sure that he was on it always. Again, we lucked out with only receiving a warning. As she handed us the warning, she nicely said, "Happy New Year."

Despite Marley's extreme athletic abilities and high energy levels, he brings us joy. He is challenging at times, but you get those quiet moments when all he wants is for you to love him. He walks up to us and will just put his head on our legs or nudge his nose under our hands so that he can get our attention. He also does the army crawl, which is funny to see. If we are across the room from him and he is lying on the floor, he will literally crawl on his belly with his back legs stretched out all the way behind him (and they look like chicken legs). Maybe he doesn't feel like walking at that moment; I don't know, but it is funny.

Marley has accumulated some loving pseudo pet names, too. We call him Miss Kitty and sometimes Prancer. Miss Kitty is because he will sit on the top of the couch just like a little kitty cat would do. He is a medium-sized dog, so it looks out of character for a dog to do that. Sometimes he sits with us like normal, but his preference is the top of the couch. My guess is that it is because he gets a bird's-eye view of everyone's business. He is called Prancer, because he is so light on his feet. When he is happy, he just floats across the floor. His walk reminds me of a Clydesdale horse with its elegant posture and prance. He must have been a dancer in his previous life. He is just light as a feather.

If You Say So, Bill

One quick, funny little note about my husband—he always says that he wants to get rid of the dogs, because we have to keep letting them out, they make a lot of noise, we always have to bail Marley out of jail, blah, blah, blah. So, he's a little bit of work. When Xena was diagnosed with her tumor, the doctor said to keep her calm. Well, having Marley in the house was not going to keep her calm by any means. Adam had to keep him at his apartment while we made arrangements for Xena.

The week Marley was gone, it was peaceful and quiet. We got to spend time with Xena without any interruptions. The doggie door was left open, and Xena could go in and out. We didn't have to keep getting up and down to let them out. We keep it closed, because Marley will jump the fence, so he has to be tethered in the yard. He can't just come and go. It was nice and a needed break for us, too. The day after Xena was gone, the house was just so quiet. It was quiet in the saddest sort of way. I can only describe it as being sort of an empty-nest syndrome. Bill came to me and said, "We have to get Marley back."

Surprised by this statement, since he always says we have to get rid of the dogs, I said, "What?"

Bill replied, "Yeah, I want the house to be protected."

"Uh-huh, right, Bill. You want him back because Marley is your TV-watching buddy who cuddles up to you or because it is you Marley crawls under the covers to sleep next to every night. I have to make reservations if I want some Billy time. Okay, you want the 'house protected.'"

Bill missed his Miss Kitty when he was gone. Needless to say, Marley was back home with us the next day terrorizing the house and our new little Joe Joe, and every day, Bill still says, "We have to get rid of the dogs."

5

Joe Joe

Joe Joe is our newest addition. He happened by chance. We were getting ready to put Xena down. The last thing we were thinking about was getting another dog. We did tell Nikki that when we lost a dog, the next one would be hers to pick out. She is now almost eleven, and having her own pet that loves her most is something I want her to experience.

Our friend Kellie, who I said earlier works at the Nevada Humane Society, came into my office and said, "There is a pug that has just arrived at the shelter. His name is Joey. He is six years old and is so fat and adorable." She knew that Nikki wanted a pug more than anything. Unsure if the timing was right because she knew that we were putting Xena down the next day, she took a chance and told me about the dog. I had her send pictures to Bill on his phone with a message saying, "Here's Nikki's new dog, Joey. When can you pick him up?" Bill didn't think it was too funny, and, as expected, he said, "No way."

Well, it was three against one, and Joey was living with us the very next day. Bill didn't stand a chance. I went down in the morning to look him over. When Nikki got out of school, she went with me to buy him. This was Nikki's very own dog. She paid for him all by herself with her own money.

The Car Ride Home

Joe Joe was very excited to be taking a car ride. That was a good sign, because we like to go places and will sometimes bring him with us. He eagerly jumped right in. Nikki and I buckled our seat belts, started the car, and almost immediately heard the window open. I knew I hadn't opened my window, because it was rather chilly outside. I looked over to Nikki's side of the car but didn't see her window down. At the same time, we both looked toward the back of the car, and Joe Joe was standing on the armrest of the back door with his paw on the window button and panting heavily with excitement. He'd rolled his own window down. He then went to the other side of the car and rolled that window down, too. I rolled up the windows to see what he would do. He went right on the armrest again and proceeded to go through the same motions as before. He opened one window and then the other, all with the biggest smile on his face. It was almost as if he knew what he was doing. Nikki and I just started cracking up. He was such a happy dog, panting in an excited fashion and smiling as he stuck his head out the window, letting the brisk January air blow into his face. Pugs tend to snort a lot. As he stuck his head out the window, Joe Joe would take a deep breath, and then a snort would come out. Breathe, snort, breathe, snort—that is what we heard all the way home.

We got Joe the day before we put down Xena. I wasn't too excited about the timing, because I didn't want Xena to be stressed. As it turns out, Xena didn't care one bit about another dog being in the house. She was always secure with her position here and knew that she was still the HDIC (Head Dog In Charge). He turned out to be quite a comfort to us after Xena was gone. He provided some comic relief as well as a meaningful first walk together.

Getting to Know Joe Joe

All of the information we had on Joe was that he was aggressive with food. When I met him, he was very friendly and didn't snap; he was just a fat, lovable dog. The first night, however, we found out that he was aggressive with a bit more than food. Joe was sleeping on our bed and on Bill's pillows. When Bill came to bed, he started picking him up to take him into Nikki's room. Joe began growling his evil-sounding little growl and then bit Bill. We all panicked a little bit. Our first thoughts were to take him back. We often have lots of kids in the house, and I didn't want anyone to get hurt. I began wondering what his past really entailed.

We decided to give him a chance and see if we could figure out why he did that. After all, he was in a new environment and wasn't used to us. Now we knew that we couldn't pick him up. So far, all else has been good. The first day we walked him, we tried to put on his harness, and he growled and snapped at me. I got it on him by offering a treat as he put his head through. It worked like a charm, and he was rewarded by going on a long walk. He now puts on the harness with no effort at all. A little patience goes a long way.

What still bothered me, though, was that Joe didn't come when I called him. I asked Kellie if that was the name he'd had before or if it was changed. The guy that brought Joe in was a friend of the person who owned him and didn't know anything about him. This is why no information was on him.

Kellie said that his name was Cujo, but the humane society couldn't put out a dog with such a name that is notorious for violent behaviors. He wouldn't stand a chance for adoption, so they renamed him Joey.

The afternoon we put Xena down, Kellie and Nancy came to our house, and we were all going to go out to the new yogurt shop down the street from our house. They wanted to try to provide some comfort to Nikki and me, so we went. It was good to get out and do something light. We talked about Joe and Nikki's excitement for having him. They had more shopping to do before they went home, and so we parted ways. Kellie called me about an hour later and said, "You're not going to believe what just happened."

She proceeded to tell me how, when they were in a store cashing out some groceries, the cashier noticed that Nancy's wallet had a Pug Saver's emblem on it. She asked Nancy if she bred pugs. Nancy said, "No, but I sure do own one."

The cashier proceeded to tell Kellie and Nancy that her friend that worked in the store just had to turn her pug in to the humane society. Both Nancy and Kellie's ears perked up, and Kellie said, "I work there. Was her pug black or fawn color?"

The girl replied, "I think it was fawn."

Kellie then asked, "Is it a girl or a boy?"

"A boy," the cashier replied. Nancy and Kellie just looked at each other.

The cashier called the girl over that turned in the pug. Kellie showed the girl the picture she had of Joe on her phone and asked her if that was her dog. She was so excited and said, "Yes!" She was happy to hear that Joe went to a good home. Nancy and Kellie told her that he was living the life and had a great home.

Kellie asked her why she gave up Joe. The girl told Kellie that she'd stolen Joe from a neighbor who'd kept him in a two-by-four-foot box. Poor Joe had been forced to sit in his own urine and feces in the box. He was never let out to exercise, which explained his weight. She was so disgusted about how he was living that she took the dog without the owner knowing and kept him. It took her six washes before

Joe no longer smelled like feces. She loved him and kept him as long as she could. She had two other large dogs and worked two jobs. The girl knew that Joe needed extra care that she couldn't give him, and she therefore did the noble thing by turning him in. She gave Kellie her number to give to us and said that if we had any questions, we could call her. I haven't done that yet but for sure will. It was really meant for Joe to be with us. It was yet another sign from God.

I could not believe the luck in finding the previous owner. Knowing Joe's background helps us to understand why he was a bit aggressive. Kellie told me to start calling him Joe Joe to see if he responds better to that. It is close to sounding like Cujo, and that is what he was called in the shelter. As he is getting used to us, he comes a little bit more often; however, we still need work in this area. Joe Joe's exercise program began on day one with the walk we used to take Xena on. To date, he has put in seven and a half miles the first week. He gets really excited when he knows that we are going for that walk. I truly believe that Joe Joe was meant to come into our lives at the exact moment he did. We saved him, and he saved us. We are now a few weeks into our relationship, but I look forward to experiencing Joe Joe's adventures in the future. Hey, I may have just named my next book.

The Dog Did It

You can't write a dog book without writing about dog farts. Now, come on, you know farts are funny every time! It doesn't matter who does it (and you all know we all do it); they are just funny. I bet everyone who has ever farted has at one time or another said, "The dog did it." Well, our little Joe Joe can clear a room in seconds. Clearly, in his short time here, he has taken the prize for the rankest-smelling farts.

For being the smallest dog we have ever had, I think Joe packs the biggest punch. They do say, after all, that big things come in little packages. He was sitting under my desk as I write this book, and lo and behold, I got the punch in the face as the pungency crept up from underneath the desk. I got up so fast and had to clear the room. He looked at me with a puzzled look as if to say, "Marley did it."

Funny Little Things He Does

It is really fun learning all of the little crazy ways about our new dog. Joe Joe has taken over Xena's kitchen spot in a big way. Xena would always supervise me in the kitchen while I cooked our meals. She would usually just stand on the sidelines and watch me work with the hopes that I would give her a tasting. Joe Joe has taken supervision to a whole new level. It appears that he is a micromanager. He literally follows me around with every step I take. If I walk to the refrigerator, he is there. If I walk to the trash can, he is there. If I walk to the sink, he is there. Joe just doesn't miss a beat. Of course, when you cook, sometimes food gets dropped. With Joe by my side, the food doesn't even hit the floor. He is like a little vacuum cleaner. It is gone before I even realize it was dropped.

We are also learning that Joe will come to us if he walks off somewhere—but he still won't come when we call his name. The other day, Bill and I were cleaning out the yard and getting it ready for spring. Joe was being good and staying in the garage. A little time had passed, and I asked Bill if Joe was still in the garage. Of course, Joe was gone. We searched the house and the yard and called out to the street—and no Joe. I went out to the front of our house and saw Joe at our neighbors' house just sniffing around. He still doesn't come when we call him all the time, so I grabbed wrapping from a food package and crinkled it so that it would make noise. Joe, recognizing this sound from the kitchen and thinking that it was food, came running in an instant. See, it is not just the dogs that can learn new tricks.

I Never Thought I Would Be One of "Those" People

We recently attended our first pug parade. It was a last minute thing and Nikki was so excited to go. Not really knowing what goes on during these events, I asked Kellie what to expect. She informed me that we should dress up Joe Joe, because he will be displayed on stage and during the parade. In a surprised voice, I replied, "Are you serious?" I never thought I would be one of "those" people who dress up their dogs. I mean, we have Akita's, St. Bernard's, and my Xena. We have never dressed up our dogs. I always felt embarrassed for the little dogs when you see them being paraded around in funny costumes. Nancy was nice enough to lend us one of Penny Lane's costumes, since we didn't have time to find one. Penny Lane, by the way, is Nancy's pug who is very experienced with this sort of thing.

Well, I am afraid to admit this, but the parade was really fun. Nikki proudly strutted across the stage with her dog. Joe Joe took the "Sure to Be a Heartbreaker" prize. Joe Joe unfortunately was dressed in Penny's lady bug costume. He did look really cute, wings and all. He even almost won the "Grand Madame" award, until the judge realized he was a boy after asking Nikki for confirmation. Oh well, you can't win them all. We are looking forward to next year's parade and you can bet he will have a really great costume.

6

Snorkey

I guess you can say that Snorkey was the beginning of my love for dogs. She was our family dog while I was growing up and was a beautiful, black Pekinese and terrier. Not to date myself here, but she was named after the character from the kids' television show *The Banana Splits* from the late sixties Whenever we took her out for walks, people always commented on what a pretty dog she was. I always felt proud. Snorkey lived to be seventeen years old, the longest of all my dogs to date.

The Middle

We lived in Philadelphia on a twelve-lane highway also known as "the Boulevard", which had a large grassy area right in the middle. Actually, we called it "the Middle." The Middle divided six lanes of road on each side. It provided everyone in the neighborhood some form of recreation, whether it was playing football, walking the dog, picking the yellow dandelions to take to your mother, or the white, delicate wishes that you blow into the air with the hope that your wish would come true. It is strange now to think of us kids playing in the middle of the highway, but that's what we did. We used to let Snorkey run her little heart out. She loved the Middle. It was a very special place for pets and people.

Every winter, we always knew that there would be huge snowstorms that would be so big that school would be cancelled the next day. Out of all of us kids, my mother was the biggest kid of them all. With Snorkey by her side, she would sit for hours in our front window that overlooked the Middle and excitedly watch the snow fall while listening to the radio waiting for the announcement that school would be closed the next day. Every flake that landed built her anticipation, because she knew that she would be waking me up from a perfectly restful slumber to make train wheels in the fresh, untouched snow. She always had to be the first one out there. Snorkey loved the snow, too, so between the two of them, I had no chance of sleeping through the night. When my nephew Bob was old enough, he, too, became part of this tradition. My brothers Jeff and David were too old for this stuff by now. Besides, waking them up was an impossible task. When she heard what she was waiting for on the radio, she had the official go-ahead to wake her kids up and let them play all night in the snow.

Midnight seemed to be the perfect time to make our train wheels. We would bundle up with layers and layers of clothes, gloves, boots, hats, and scarves and head outside into the quiet, peaceful winter air. Amazingly, the Boulevard by day is a totally different animal than at night. During the day, literally thousands of cars rush by to get to their destinations. Rush hour was always between four o'clock and six o'clock at night; by nighttime, it is slow, quiet, and lulling. When it snowed, it always seemed to be even more silent. When a car went by, it just had a slow *whooshing* sound that you could almost meditate by. A new car would pass by, and again the *whoosh* . . . and another *whoosh*. It was rhythmic and soothing. That peacefulness would only last until my mom reached the perfect destination.

"Let the train wheels begin!" She would start the circle, and the kids would follow. Snorkey tagged right along with us. The snow was usually too high for her, so she followed our footsteps just as Xena followed Nana's. Her tail would be wagging, tongue out while panting from the cold and excitement building with each step. Time always stood still during those moments, and we loved every minute of it.

When it was time to go back home, we always made hot chocolate and continued watching the snow fall from our window. Snorkey's paws were always loaded with balls of ice, so we quickly got her warmed up by rubbing her down with a big towel and removing the ice balls from her feet. It doesn't take money to have family fun. All you need is lots of love, heavy snowfall, a crazy mother, and a great dog.

Waiting For the Tooth Fairy

As I said earlier, Snorkey lived to be seventeen years old, which is just amazing. She lived longer than any other dog I have ever had. Of course, just as with humans, as you age, teeth become less productive and eventually fall out. This was certainly the case with Snorkey. I always knew when she lost another tooth, because just as the sun will rise each morning, so, too, will Snorkey loose her teeth in my bed. It was gross. My brothers used to think that it was a riot. I didn't. That is, until I had an idea. I could maybe make a bit of money if I put her tooth under my pillow.

I gave it a go. I was not sure if it would work, since I never heard of the Tooth Fairy giving money for dog teeth, but it was worth a shot. I wrapped her brown, rotten tooth up in toilet paper, just as I wrapped my teeth, although mine were not rotten. The next morning, I awoke with excitement with the hopes of seeing a shiny coin under my pillow. I already had the money spent. I wanted to get a peanut butter Tandycake from the corner store. They are my favorite. I was even going to share with Snorkey, because she was a peanut butter fan, too, and after all, it was her tooth.

Well, to my surprise, there was no money to be found. I tried and tried with each tooth, but I never had any success. Luckily, the Tooth Fairy still came for my teeth.

Snorkey and I walked down to the corner store together. As she waited outside for me just as she always had before, I purchased our peanut buttery treat, and we ate it along the walk home together. She aggressively licked the roof of her mouth to make sure that she had gotten every delicious morsel, and I was enjoying every moment with her.

Grandmom and Bazooka Bubblegum

My grandparents used to own a newspaper stand underneath the El Station on Frankford Avenue in Philadelphia. They sold all types of papers, magazines, cigarettes, and all of the different types of candy you could possibly imagine. I used to love visiting her there, because she always let me pick out candy. Grandmom always had candy in her purse, too, and best of all, when we visited her each week at her house, the first thing she'd ask was if we wanted some candy. "Go and get some candy in the frigidaire, doll." She always called us "doll," and I don't really know why she called the refrigerator the "Frigidaire", but she did. Perhaps that was the model she had. I didn't care what she called it. All I cared about was what was inside. Her vegetable drawers were always stocked to the brim with M&Ms, Snickers, Hershey bars, 5th Avenues—all the good stuff. It was a little piece of heaven on earth, and it was all in my Grandmom's "refridgadaire".

Every week, my grandparents came to our house for a family dinner. Grandmom also always had a fair share of Bazooka bubblegum in her purse. The Bazooka and Tootsie Rolls were Snorkey's favorite. We both looked forward to family dinner night. My parents never really let us have very much candy in the house, so it was always a treat when Grandmom came over.

I remember one particular Friday night visit, Grandmom was sitting on the couch, and everyone was having some good adult conversations with each other. I was on the floor next to where Grandmom was sitting sort of hiding and being shy. I wanted to ask her for gum but was afraid. Snorkey was never afraid to ask. She was sitting in front of Grandmom just staring and looking pretty as she always did, practically expecting Grandmom to ask her if she wanted some bubblegum. I knew if I hung around Snorkey, Grandma would eventually notice her glaring stare and give her a piece; then, of course, she would ask me if I wanted one. It was a win-win situation. Grandmom used to get a kick out of feeding Snorkey bubblegum. I loved that dog. I loved that she loved her Bazooka bubblegum, and I loved Grandmom for always being prepared.

Mom's Home

My mom used to work for the Philadelphia Fire Department. It was all the way downtown. She had to take the bus and El train to get there. Every day, she got off the bus across the Boulevard at almost exactly 5:30 every night. Snorkey and her internal clock anxiously awaited by the front windows, looking for Mom across the street. In the summertime, our windows would be open, and when she saw Mom get off the bus, Snorkey would start singing so loudly that my mom could hear her across the twelve-lane highway. Sometimes, others would get off the bus with her and wonder about the barking dog. Mom would have to explain it was her dog and that it was our routine every day.

Snorkey and I would then go outside and sit on our steps. I would hold her tightly, because she would run into the rush-hour traffic to be with Mom. As my mom got closer and closer to our side of the street, I would whisper in an excited voice into Snorkey's ear, "Here she comes! Here comes Mommy!" This, of course, elevated Snorkey's excitement to a fever pitch. It was like winding up a toy and letting it go. The second my mom put her foot on the sidewalk on our side of the street, I let Snorkey go, and she took off like a bolt of lightning, her tail wagging and her little butt swinging joyfully from side to side as she ran to greet Mom. It was always a happy sight to see. We all looked forward to when Mom came home.

It is the little moments in our pets' lives that we should remember and treasure always. It doesn't take much to make them happy.

The Water Ice Truck

Being a kid in our Philly neighborhood was fun. We lived in row homes, and in between the long row of houses was our driveway and then another set of row homes. I think there were about thirty houses in a block. The driveway was where all of the action took place. We played kickball, basketball, and Buck Buck, jumped rope, roller skated, hung out—you name it, we played it. It was where all of the kids gathered together and played.

One of my favorite memories as a kid was when the water ice truck came down our street.

The driver would start ringing his bell before he got onto our street, and all of the kids started screaming, *"Water ice!"* We all scattered like roaches to ask our parents for fifty cents so that we could get a water ice and a soft pretzel. Snorkey would hear the bell and start barking with excitement, because she knew what was coming. Sometimes getting money from my mom was tough, because the water ice guy always came right before dinnertime. Once my mom said no, I would go sit on my dad's lap and bat my eyes. I had to do the begging quickly, because I didn't want the truck to leave without making my purchase. My dad was always a softy and said yes. When I got the money, Snorkey and I would run back to the water ice truck with anticipation, get in line, and then place our order for a chocolate water ice and a soft pretzel. It was the best! Snorkey's tail always stood up in an alert fashion, and she would briskly walk me back to our part of the driveway, constantly looking at me while I licked my water ice. It was as if she was saying, "Hey, don't forget me." All of the kids would be sitting together, and I would have my dog sharing my tasty treats with me. Treats always taste better when you have someone to share them with.

I haven't thought of Snorkey this much in quite a while. She has been gone from this world a long time, and now when I think of her, I don't feel the pain of her being gone; I feel the warmth and love of my childhood friend who will always be in my heart. Her stories make me reminiscent of my childhood and how easy things were back then. I think that is what she represents to me now. She was my friend and my constant companion. I feel warm and cozy when I think about water ice, Bazooka bubblegum, and Snorkey.

7

Meisha

Her Long Journey

Meisha was my mom's dog, but her story of how she came to be a part of our family is worth telling. My mom had come to Reno for a visit. She was still living in Philly but was planning to move to Reno to be closer to me. She had always loved shih tzu dogs and used to say that one day she would get one. While she was here, I came across someone that needed to give away his dog, because he was no longer able to care for her. The dog was a shih tzu named Shu Shu. Of course, with the opportunity such as this coming up, I had no choice but to take the dog. I surprised my mom, and she was so excited to have her. It was a good fit, and both were very happy with the new friendship.

As I said, Mom was going to move out to Reno, but she had to go home again, pack her house up, and sell it. She flew home, and Shu Shu flew with her. The dog adjusted well but was a bit wild. My mom still lived on the Boulevard, the twelve-lane highway. It was infamous for hitting many dogs, as they run out of their houses and try to get to the Middle. One day, Mom's gate was not shut tightly. Shu Shu ran out the door before my mom even knew what was going on. She flew out the gate and ran right into the rush-hour traffic. She was killed immediately.

Mom called me up right away, hysterically crying. I felt so badly that I could not be there to comfort her. Her neighbors and friends were there and helped her get through her loss. For the next few days, she was so down and depressed. She felt guilty and wished that she could turn back time. She felt bad that I had given her the dog, and now it was gone. I told her that it was not her fault. I knew that I had to do something, and I told Bill that we needed to find her another dog. She was talking about getting another one. I immediately called her friend Rose, who lived down the street. I told Rose to not let her buy another dog. I said, "Tell her to wait until she gets to Reno and settles down before she looks for one."

Bill and I started scouring the newspapers for anyone selling shih tzu dogs. We searched every day for two weeks, and finally Bill found some for sale. The only problem was that they were in Sacramento, California. It is only a two-hour drive, but was that something we wanted to do—or should we wait for something local to come up? We were not sure what to do. Bill said, "We have no choice." She needed a dog and needed one now. He loves Mom and always did whatever he could for her. He did all of the arranging, called to schedule a visit with the dogs, purchased it, and, with Adam holding Meisha on his lap, drove her home.

We didn't tell my mom that he was coming or anything about the dog. I did tell her that I was sending her a package, and it should be arriving the next day. A surprise would do her good right about now. Bill arranged a flight to Philly with the new puppy that he had fallen in love with. When he got to Philly, he rented a car and drove straight to Mom's house. With dog in hand, he excitedly knocked on the door. He couldn't wait for her to get her surprise. Well, he knocked and knocked, and there was no answer. He saw lights on upstairs in her room, so he knew that she was home. Frustrated, he walked all the way down to the corner store, which was about a half of a city block, to use the phone to call me. This was before cell phones were everywhere. He told me that he saw lights but that she was not answering.

I told him to go back and that I would call her. She answered the phone, and I began a casual conversation as we always do. I asked how she was feeling, and of course, she was still moping around and feeling sad and lonely without Shu Shu.

I asked, "Did you ever get the package I sent you?"

She replied, "No, what is it?"

I asked again, "Did you check the front door? Maybe it was left there."

She said that she hadn't but that she would check it in the morning. She had just gone upstairs and didn't want to go down again. There were a lot of steps in the house, and it had become hard for her to go up and down them. I forcefully told her to go. "I think I hear someone at your door. Don't you hear knocking?" I asked.

She said, "What are you talking about?"

Telling her a little white lie, I said, "I called the company about the package, and they said it would be there tonight." I told her to go check.

Mom was a slow mover, so it took her some time to get downstairs. I could hear Bill knocking, and in the background, I heard my mom yell at the door, "Wait a minute, wait a minute! I'm coming." She opened the door, and all she saw was this little, furry black-and-white dog being held out in front of her face. She couldn't see who was holding her until Bill peeked around the side of the dog. All I heard on the phone was the biggest, most excited scream I have ever heard. "What is this? How did you get here? Oh, my goodness!" She went on and on. I could hear the joy and her spirit lift immediately. I was smiling from ear to ear, because I felt that she was getting the relief she needed after mourning the loss of Shu Shu.

She held that dog so tightly, kissing and loving it. Meisha came a long way to find her new person. It took her a two-hour drive from Sacramento to Reno, an eight-hour flight from Reno to Philly, a forty-five minute drive to the house, and finally into the arms of her new mommy. This made Meisha's story that much more special. She lived to be twelve years old. It was worth traveling all of those miles. She had the best life, and she was so loved by all of us. She was the best dog my mom ever had. It's amazing how the universe works. Those pets that are to be together with us will always find a way, because that is what is meant to be.

Conclusion

I hope you've enjoyed the stories of our beloved pets as much as I've enjoyed reliving and sharing them with you. It has helped with my own healing process. Being with our pets through their lives and their deaths is a gift and an honor. That is what I hope you take away from reading this book. As I was writing this book, so many people began telling me their own pet stories. You see their faces light up as they describe the scenes and events in the stories. It's as if for only a moment they get all warm inside just thinking about them. Animals fulfill needs in all of us. They are to be cherished. Don't forget to enjoy them and all of the noise they make in your house. I promise you that it will be missed when they are gone. Please remember to visit your local humane society, donate your time when possible, and, most of all, do what is right by your pets. They only know how to love and ask for nothing in return but for you to love them back. What more can we ask for?

Adam & Sumo

Nikki & Sumo

Sumo pup

Hampshire pup

Hampshire & Taz

Joe

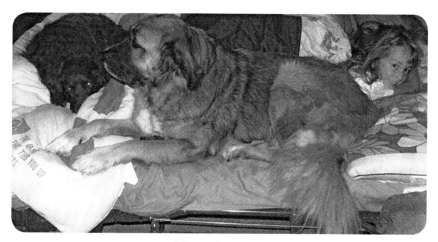

Nana & Xena

Marley & Joe waking Nikki up for school.

Baby face Marley

Nikki & Baby Marley

Xena & Marley

Love that Face

Water Dog

Xena letting Marley win

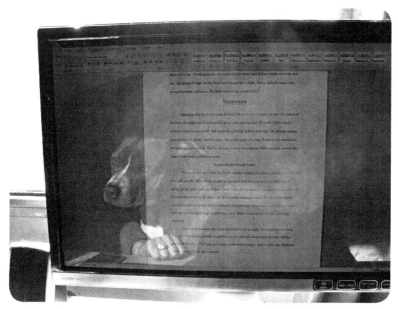

Marley at computer

Xena & Babies

Kiss, kiss

Buds

Marley and his boy Adam

Bill, Nikki, & Xena hiking Squaw

Roe, Bill, Nikki & Xena at the top of Squaw. "We made it"

CPSIA information can be obtained at www.ICGtesting.com
Printed in the USA
BVOW011308290911

272351BV00001B/137/P

9 781463 409326